+

HYPNOSIS - 201

ADVANCED TECHNIQUES

BY

Larry M. McDaniel

ISBN: 978-1-300-80003-3

FOREWORD

The purpose of this course is to enhance the skills of the beginning therapist. It doesn't deal with basics but enhances advanced techniques and practices designed to induce a subject in the hypnotic state for therapy preparation.

This course doesn't cover hypnotherapy, hynoanalysis or any other involved and complex therapy procedure but will enhance the skill of the beginner and give insight into achievement of access to the subconscious mind for positive beginnings. Some progress toward habit control and personal improvement programs will be presented along with advanced self-hypnosis techniques and problem solving methods. It is assumed that the student will be far enough along from the previous beginning course to comprehend this material and utilize and incorporate in into his consciousness for further assimilation and perfection of his ability to be of help to his fellow man.

This course is presented in an outline form for easy reference and as a teaching aid. Clear instructions as to these advanced procedures are given for good understanding on the part of the student.

BACKGROUND

The author, Mr. Larry M. McDaniel, holds a BA Degree in Psychology from Oglethorpe University in Atlanta, Georgia. His post-graduate studies in Advanced Psychotherapeutic Analysis were done through the University of Southern California's Continuing Education Program that was administered through the facilities of the American Institute of Hypnosis headquartered in Los Angeles, California. William Jennings Bryan, Jr., M.D., Ph.D., LLD, and JD headed this foundation. Dr. Bryan also headed up the College of Medical Hypnosis during the 1970's until his death in the mid-70's. Mr. McDaniel was trained thoroughly in all phases of medical hypnosis and was admitted to the faculty of the American Institute of Hypnosis in 1969. He taught MD's and Ph.D. level students until the mid 1970's.

The author has been a guest on TV and radio shows in the Atlanta, Georgia area as well as other parts of the nations and was the keynote speaker at the annual meeting of the American Polygraph Association in 1971. He has taught thousands of medical and psychological personnel as well as lay people the art and science of hypnosis through the American Institute and later through his own "American Institute for human Development in Atlanta, Georgia. He was certified by the State of Georgia Merit System in 1976 as Clinical Psychologist. He was also the Founder and past president of the National Hypnotherapy Association that was headquartered in Atlanta, Georgia.

TABLE OF CONTENTS

CHAPTER ONE

ADDITIONAL DEFINITIONS OF HYPNOSIS

As the student progresses into further study of hypnosis, he must become familiar with additional theories, definitions and new understandings of hypnosis. The researchers presented herein are but a few of the many giants who have come before us and made concerted efforts to describe the hypnotic phenomena.

McDougal: "Voluntary attention is withdrawn from the outer world and concentrated in force upon the vasomotor system, producing changes impossible in normal

circumstances."

Bryan, William J.: "Hypnosis a normal physiological, altered state of

consciousness, similar to but not the same as being

awake; similar to but not the same as being asleep, and

is produced by the presence of two conditions: (1) A

central focus of attention, and (2) surrounding areas of

inhibition. The state of hypnosis, in turn produces

three things: (1) An increased concentration of the

mind, (2) An increased relaxation of the body, and (3)

An increased susceptibility to suggestion."

Fross, Garland: "Controlled Daydreaming"

Erickson, Milton: "Erickson includes both the subject and hypnotist in

the description. When he speaks of "hypnosis" he is

not merely referring to the process within a subject

but to the type of interchange between two people.

Consequently, his emphasis is upon the hypnotist

gaining cooperation from the subject, dealing with

resistant behavior, receiving acknowledgement that
something is happening, and so on.   It is this broader
definition of hypnosis which makes it difficult at
times to tell whether Erickson hypnotized a patient
or not. He used a type of interchange which he con-
siders hypnotic although no formal induction of
hypnosis in the traditional sense was conducted. his
introduction of two people into the definition of
hypnosis requires a new formulation of that age-old
phenomenon."

Kroger, William S.   "The processing storage and retrieval of
information in hypnosis can be understood better
from the study of brain-machine (computer)
analogies. The brain acts in hypnosis according to
the same principles set down by the physical sciences
for the design of communication equipment. Thus,
greater receptivity (produced by fixation of attention,
relaxation and concentration) in a receptor (the
subject) enables messages (sensory inputs or

percepts, i.e., information) to be received clearly

from a transmitter (the operator) with a minimal

degree of interference (noise), either in the external

environmental communications pathways (channel)

or in the internal sensory receptors of the subject.

This allows greater self-objectivity and self-

exploration of the subjective thoughts, feelings and

attitudes. Thus, hypnosis is an adaptive response

mechanism which enhances the transmission of ideas

and their understanding in a more effective manner

than at ordinary walking levels, at which attention

is scattered."

PAVLOV: "In other words, the mere mention of a word

associated with a certain physiological reaction elicits

that reaction even though the original stimulus has

been forgotten. Thus, a word does not become

meaningful until a conditioned reflex between it and

some conditioned or unconditioned stimulus takes

place in the cortex. For instance, in the child, the

word 'hurt' acquires a definite meaning only after it

has been associated with real pain. After that, the appropriate conditioned reaction to the word 'hurt' can be evoked to reproduce the exact conditioned (pain reaction) response. Once a conditioned reflex is established, the person automatically reacts without thinking to nongenuine stimulus that has become part of the reflex. In the example just given this would be the word 'hurt'."

Ullman, Leonard P. and Krasner, Leonard: "Hypnosis is conceptualized as a role-taking phenomena involving an individual performing behaviors in response to the demand characteristics supplied in the 'hypnotic' situation. The major implication of this view is that hypnosis, like abnormal behavior, follows the rules of normal behavior and is not discontinuous with it. No new laws need e postulated to explain hypnosis."

Hilgard, E. R.: "Without attempting a formal definition of hypnosis, the field appears well enough specified by the increased suggestibility of the subject following induction procedures stressing relaxation, free play of imagination, and the withdrawal of reality

supports through closed eyes, narrowing of

attention, and concentration on the voice of the

hypnotist."

The student will gradually assimilate a definition of his own as he

progresses through greater levels of understanding of this phenomena.

These have been presented for a greater study and awareness.

CHAPTER TWO

THEORIES

A.   Analysts:

1.   Ferenczi: Transference - Hypnotist becomes mother or father,

subject regresses to infantile level.

2.   Gill and Brenman: "Hypnosis is a particular kind of regressive

process which may be initiated either by sensorimotor

ideational deprivation or by the stimulation of an archaic

relationship to the hypnotist...when the regressive process has been set into motion by either one of these two kids of factors,

phenomena characteristic of the other kind begin to emerge."

B. Altered State Views:

1. Subjective deviation from normal waking experience of

    psychological functioning.

2. A. M. Ludvig: Characteristics - Alteration in thinking, time sense,

    perception, body image (depersonalization), suggestibility.

3. Relinquish conscious control, extreme expression of emotions,

    inability to describe.

4. Function: (a). Maladaptive - escape mechanism

    Inadvertent (highway hypnosis)

    (b) Adaptive - healing, pleasure, night, social

    needs.

C.   WEAK STATE THEORIST:

1. Hilgard - 50% variance is accounted for the by characteristics of

    the subject.

2.   Orne   - "Hypnosis is said to exist when suggestions from

one individual seemingly alter the perception and memories of

another."

(a) Demand Characteristics.

(b) Differences between wake and hypnotic behavior:

    (1). Subjective reports

    (2). Subtle behavior - source amnesia

    (3). Trance logic.

D. BEHAVIORIST APPROACH (Skeptical - contiguous with normal)

    1. Sarbin, Theodore - Role enactment "Modern Theory sees the hypnotic interaction as continuous with other social interactions...hypnosis, on this view, is not a special "state" of the organism. The behaviors are artifacts of the role as pre-Scribed by the experimenter and interpreted By the subject." Enactment of role produces concomitant physiological changes.

E. PSYSIOLOGICAL APPROACHES:

1. Sarbin, Theodore - Byproduct of role enactment - "Shifts in cerebral circulation occur as a by-product on the somnolence or the emotional excitement...(which) in turn allows subcortical centers to achieve temporary dominance so that behavior mediated by the subcortex and the autonomic nervous system may be observed."

2. Pavlov   "Inhibition, ordinary sleep and hypnosis are one and the same process."

3. David Akstein -   Reticular formation allowing activation of specific sites of cortex. Diffuse cortical inhibition with selective activation by reticular formation.

4. DiCara and Miller - Hypnosis decreases internal noise allowing efficient learning of autonomic control.

CHAPTER THREE

HYPNOTIC MANAGEMENT

DEEPENING:

THE GENERAL PRINCIPLE:

The main purpose for additional techniques involving a greater accessibility to the subconscious is to assist the subject to make maximum utilization of the effort at improvement. Having access to a greater receptivity in the subconscious significantly affords both the hypnotist and the subject a greater response to applied efforts.

PROCEDURES:

The main procedure is to first ascertain the depth at which you are working. Tests may need to be made to determine the level at which your subject has reached and also as to the method of deepening you will use.

You will not use an authoritative approach when you have a defiant or resistant subject and you certainly would not want to use permissive techniques with a very submissive subject.

With the resistant subject, a very effective technique is to allow him to relax his arm to such a degree that he cannot lift it. The technique is as follows:

"You are now very relaxed. Very, very, relaxed. Notice how relaxed you are. Notice how relaxed your right arm is now. Notice how very relaxed your right arm is. Now allow your right arm to become so relaxed that it feels almost detached from your body. Allow your right arm to become so relaxed that you can't move it. Try to lift it and you will find that you cannot move it. When you have allowed it to become relaxed so much that you can't move it, try to lift it and you will find that you can't lift it. You can't lift it because you have allowed it to relax so much that you can't lift it. Test yourself, test yourself and be sure that you can't lift your arm.

If your subject does manage to lift his arm, tell him to relax himself further. Have him relax himself to the point that he cannot raise his arm on another try. This places the hypnotic depth squarely on the shoulders of the subject. He will determine his own depth and feel that he is in complete control. Continued practice of this technique will greatly enhance your success with difficult subjects and enable you to carry on with your work with much greater effectiveness.

COMPOUNDING SUGGESTIONS:

When you have someone relaxed, you will want to use wording that emphasizes compounded depth. Wording such as, "You are going twice as deep as before...with each number you are going twice as deep as before..."

Repeating phrases emphasizing that your subject will go twice as deep every time he hears a certain word or sees a certain elevator or staircase enhances his perception of his own mental receptivity as going "deeper" within.

When you bring your subject out of each session it is well to suggest that each time he re-enters the hypnotic state that he will go twice as deep as before. The continual repetition of the deepening suggestions will reinforce your subject's ability to enter the subconscious to an increasingly greater degree.

A. GENERAL PRINCIPLES FOR DEEPENING:

1. The more you can predict future actions, the greater will be your subject's compliance.

2, The more your subject follows instructions, the greater the depth.

E.g., motor movements, analgesia, etc.

B. PROCEDURES;

    1. Almost any induction method can be used for deepening.

    2. Counting - have your subject imagine a blackboard on which he writes the number 100. He then erases the number and writes the next lower number, i.e. 99, 98. etc. He continues until he reaches 0.

    3. Elevator: The Subject imagines that he is on an elevator on the 20th floor as the hypnotist counts down from 20 to 0.

        a. As he watches the numbers decrease, he feels himself going lower and lower, going at a steady speed.

        b. Hypnotist lowers his voice as he reports the lower floors.

    4. Compounding Suggestions

        a. Tell your subject that he will be twice as relaxed each time he opens and closes his eyes.

        b. Have your subject stare into your eyes for a second and then close them.

        c. Reward your subject - "Good, you are very relaxed."

        d. Tell your subject to count backward from 100 and with each number he counts, he will get twice as relaxed.

e. Tell your subject that when he gets to 98 all numbers will

disappear.

5. Challenge Methods

a. Advantage - Successful completion is a dramatic proof that

your subject has actually been in hypnosis.

b. Disadvantages:

1. Failure ruins confidence in the hypnotist.

2. Failure decreases hypnotic depth.

c. Examples:

1. See that you cannot bend your rigid arm.

2. See that you cannot unclasp your fingers.

3. See that you cannot open your eyes.

CHAPTER FOUR

LECRON-BORDEAUX SCORING SYSTEM OF HYPNOTIC DEPTH

There are many ways of measuring hypnotic depth. We use twelve stages as illustrated in the basic Hypnosis Course 101. Many hypnotists use only three stages and some use as many as one hundred. For practical purposes, twelve is quite sufficient. The Aron measure is six stages and it is called the "Master Depth Rule". They are mentioned here for your reference and information.

LECRON-BORDEAUX SCORING SYSTEM FOR INDICATING DEPTH OF HYPNOSIS

DEPTH	SCORE	Symptoms and Phenomena
Unsusceptible	0	Subject fails to react
Hynoidal	1.	Physical Relaxation

	2.	Drowsiness apparent
	3.	Fluttering of eyelids
	4.	Closing of eyes
	5.	Mental lethargy
	6.	Heaviness of limbs
Light Trance	7.	Catalepsy of eyes
	8.	Partial limb catalepsy
	9.	Small muscle inhibition
	10.	Deep, slow breathing
	11.	Disinclination to move
	12.	Twitching of jaw - mouth
	13.	Subject; operator rapport
	14.	Post-hyp. response.
	15.	eye twitch upon wakeup
	16.	Personality changes
	17.	Bodily heaviness
	18.	Some detachment feeling
Medium Trance	19.	Recognition of trance
	20.	Total muscle inhibition
	21.	Partial amnesia

24

	22.	Glove anesthesia
	23.	Tactile Illusions
	24.	Gustatory Illusions
	25.	Olfactory Illusions
	26.	Hyperacuity to environmental conditions
	27.	Body catalepsy
Deep or Somnambulistic Trance	28.	In-trance eye opening
	29.	Eyes have fixed stare
	30.	Somnambulism
	31.	Partial Anesthesia
	32.	Post-Hypnotic sugg.
	33.	Complete Anesthesia
	34.	Post-Hyp. Anesthesia
	35.	Bizarre Post-Hyp. suggestions heeded
	36.	Eye coordination lost
	37.	Detached feelings
	38.	Rigidity in muscles
	39.	Hypnotist fades in/out

	40.	Control blood pressure
	41.	Age Regression
	42.	Revivification
	43.	+ visual hallucination
	44.	- visual hallucination
	45.	+Auditory "
	46.	-Auditory "
	47.	Dream stimulation
	48.	Hyperesthesias
	49	Color sensations
Planary Trance	50.	Stuporous condition in which all activity is inhibited.

ARON'S MASTER DEPTH RULE

FIRST STAGE: Muscle relaxation - Eye catalepsy - subject cannot open his eyelids if told he cannot.

SECOND STAGE: Muscle catalepsy - Subject cannot move isolated groups of muscles, such as arms or legs.

THIRD STAGE: Subject's arms can be made "Stiff and rigid as a steel bar". He cannot rise from chair if told that he cannot.

FOURTH STAGE: Here, there is true amnesia. The subject will FORGET the number between 5 and 7. He will retain sense of touch but feel no pain.

FIFTH STAGE: Positive visual and auditory hallucinations, complete anesthesia and post hypnotic.

SIXTH STAGE: Negative hallucinations.

CATALEPSY: Occurs in first three stages.

AMNESIA: Cannot SAY number between 5 and 7 in the Third Stage. Cannot REMEMBER number between 5 and 7 in the Fourth Stage.

ANESTHESIA: Can feel touch but no pain in Fourth Stage. Can feel nothing in Fifth and Sixth Stages.

HALLUCINATIONS: Positive in Fifth Stage. Negative in Sixth.

All of these phenomena occur as a result of suggestions, not spontaneously.

CHAPTER FIVE

AGE REGRESSION

The purpose of age regression is to enable the subject to re-experience the original causative factor leading to the problem at hand. If your subject suffers from a lack of concentration, there was a starting point for this distraction. Through regression we can help the subject pinpoint the original feeling or experience of frustration or diversion of concentration which resulted in continual mind wandering whenever he tried to study or concentrate from that point on.

The type of regression we want is not a "memory" type of description from the subject but rather a "reliving" type of experience. Rather than have your subject simply describe an event to us from conscious memory, we want the subject to be there mentally as though he were actually there. We want him to be able to re-experience the actual feelings and thoughts that were experienced at that particular time. Once the original pattern has been discovered and the subject relives it, then corrective suggestions can be given that will enable him to release the past emotional hold that the situation has represented and exchange it for a more positive attitudinal approach.

Many times we suffer from fears and personal problems which arose from childhood experiences that we interpreted as being a threat to our sense of well being from a child's point of view but which now we would not judge to be so. If you were in a pillow fight with your brother or sister and happened to have been sufficiently suffocated to the point of fearing for your life you well may suffer from asthma from that day on. Once the fear is remembered and released, your asthma goes with it.

Many problems are easily discovered but many are not so easy to discern. Birth traumas, heavily repressed fears stemming from abusive parents and other sources are so repressed that it requires extensive analysis to uncover the causative material to the point where it can be dealt with and the problem either solved or helped to a significant degree.

Regression to the point of reliving is known as "Revivification". The reaction that sometimes occurs during the revivification is known as the "Abreaction". Your subject may well scream and react as though the feared thing is upon him again. When this happens, the operator continues to talk in a confident manner and enables his subject to actually intensify the fear, relive the trauma and then release it from his subject's mind to the point that it no longer has any hold on him.

There are many methods of enabling our subject to enter a regressive state deep enough for revivification to occur. Generally, any good deepening technique will enhance the depth enough to begin work in this area. However, there are other techniques that are exclusively designed to enable you to assist your subject of discovery of past events.

TECHNIQUES FOR REGRESSION:

1. Railroad Method: Have your subject board a train and watch sign posts as the train moves. Ask your subject to see the sign posts become mile-markers and then year-markers as the train takes him back into the past. When he arrives at the proper year, have the train stop and the subject can then exit the train and you can begin the therapy.

2. Time Methods: Ask your subject to visualize the hands of a grandfather clock moving backward. Ask him to see the hands move backward faster and faster until your subject has been transported

back in time to the proper time period.

3.   Modified Implosive Feeling Method: Ask your subject to focus on the feelings of fear, tension or problem that he wants corrected. Have him feel it to such an increasing degree that he can isolate it and describe it in detail. Continue to magnify the feeling as much as possible and then have him return in time to the first time he felt that way. Once the causative factor has been identified, have your subject release any and all fear, anxiety or problems associated with that particular event.

Regression is one of the most dynamic methods of problem clarification available to the hypnotherapist. Through regression, you can get to the core of the problem and clear it without long and protracted visits. Once the core of the problem has been cleared, the rest is simply applied positive suggestions.

Many hypnotherapists do not use regression but do use only applied positive suggestions. Positive suggestions are effective in many cases and will result in notable improvements, especially for the short term. However, if your weight person does lose weight but does not deal with the true cause of the overweight condition, he or she will return to the obese condition after a short period of time. Positive suggestion therapy is good for mild to light problems but is not effective for long-term or difficult problems.

There is a process that is designed especially to discover the hidden or subconscious cause of problems. This method is known as "Hypnoanalysis" and deals with recognition of subconscious language, word association testing and dreams. Hypnoanalysis is the final culmination of hypnosis training and will enable the practitioner to deal with the total picture of the problem and effectively help the subject to clarify his or her problem permanently.

CHAPTER SIX

AUTOMATIC WRITING

When your subject has achieved the deeper stages of hypnosis, you can then employ the technique of automatic writing to discover causes of problems which are not available to the subject's conscious memory or are too unpleasant to face. By the use of automatic writing you will be able to unearth many facts which will be helpful in your subject's therapy.

In age regression you can have your subject give you a sample of handwriting at each state of the regression. You will find that as he gets younger, the handwriting changes and will match that of his earlier writing styles.

Testing your subject's handwriting is one method of determining if your subject is actually regressed to the point of reliving the event or is simply "remembering". If he is remembering the event the handwriting show no changes. However, if your subject is reliving a time in the past at the age of ten, the handwriting will reflect this and appear to be that of a ten-year-old child. The next step to testing the handwriting is automatic writing.

When your subject is deeply hypnotized and capable of regression and handwriting changes, have him imagine that his right (or left) arm is now detached from his body and that he cannot control it any longer. Have your subject visualize himself on the beach or at some other pleasant location while his right arm is totally free and able to write and answer any question that you may ask. Tell him that the arm will answer totally honestly and will withhold no answer to any questions. Tell him that he will not be concerned with what the arm answers and, indeed, will not be aware of any answers that it may write.

When this procedure has been performed, you may proceed with your questions. Have a pencil and pad ready for the responses and make your questions clear and simple.

CHAPTER SEVEN

ADDTIONAL FACTORS

A.   ADVANCED TECHNIQUES

1.) Weight Control: Weight problems stem from feelings of emptiness resulting from a lack of love, attention or affection experienced at a young age. Invariably, you will find that the point of origin is when the child perceives a loss of love from one or other parent and substitutes "sweets" for love. There are other factors, of course, but this is the main one you will have to deal with.

Weight problems require a lot of reinforcement. If your subject does not cooperate and expects to lose weight simply because he was hypnotized , your results will be nil. Remember, any therapy is a two-way street requiring efforts on the part of the subject as well as the hypnotherapist.

2.) Smoking: Smoking originates as a need to be accepted by peers. this usually manifests at age twelve to fifteen or so. When your subject begins smoking it is often only a few cigarettes per day.

However, as the stress of life kicks in, the habit rapidly increases to one or two packs per day. Additional stress, such as divorce, job stress, etc., tends to cause the habit to increase it even beyond two packs per day.

The basic problem with smoking is that most people fight the habit of smoking and don't realize what they have associated with the habit of smoking. Once they relieve the associations with acceptance of smoking and believe that they can quit and make an effort, your success will be quite high.

It must be noted here that smoking is a physical addiction caused by the ingestion of nicotine. This physical craving will require about three days of total abstinence from smoking. Once that milestone has been reached your job will be much easier.

3.) Concentration Improvement: Concentration blockages result from distractions experienced in grammar school associated with anger, sexual frustration, mind wandering, general immaturity and other factors. Regression back to the first time he had trouble concentrating and releasing the tension, frustration, fixation or whatever the distraction was will result in your subject's ability to concentrate much more effectively.

Once the blockage is removed, apply positive suggestions

for correction and the school grades will dramatically improve.

4.)Memory Blockages: Fear of public speaking, sales blocks

and many other problems of a similar nature can be taken care

of in the same manner as the procedure dealing with

concentration mentioned above.

5.) Introductory Sexual Therapy: Sexual problems are

generally more involved and will require extensive analysis

including word-association testing, dream analysis and

regression. Much sexual therapy is needed for sexual

sublimations, repression, perversions and other problems

related to the reproductive drive.

Sexual problems, such as pedophilia, homosexuality,

voyeurism, impotence, frigidity and other troublesome

problems can, in many cases, be effectively dealt with though

properly administered hypnotherapy. There are some cases that

no matter what you do; your client will show no improvement.

This is when he or she should be referred for additional care to

other professionals.

6.) Self-Hypnosis: Self-hypnosis techniques are very effective once your subject has been helped to overcome his problem. Since the subject has been in hypnosis several times, it will be a natural thing for you to post-hypnotically condition him to self-hypnosis.

Once your subject has mastered self-hypnosis he can reinforce your help and continue to build self-programming for his own improvement realizations.

B. SUBLIMINAL PROGRAMMING

1.) Subliminal programming is the process of placing hypnotic suggestions "behind" or "beneath" the normal level of awareness. By playing music and recording subliminal messages either by accelerated voice overlaid on top of the music or by high speed messages intermixed with the music, we are supposed to become conditioned without having to go through the conscious mind. The subconscious is supposed to be able to act upon the suggestions.

Subliminal programming is controversial. Many feel that no results are obtained while others swear by it. The only thing that is certain is that it can act as a placebo. If the subject expects it to work - it will.

Subliminal messages are usually done through tapes. The music is loud and clear and the subliminal message can barely be heard if at all.

People can make their own subliminal tapes by recording music and the recording suggestions on top of the music if they have the proper equipment. However, the professionally done tapes usually can be purchased reasonably and are better done that the homemade variety.

Commercial applications are being felt in some of the retail markets where subliminal programs have been played to the customers in the stores. Some claims have been made that shoplifting has been reduced by as much as 30%. Whether this is a sales pitch or fact might be difficult to determine.

C: LUCID DREAMING

1.) A good hypnotic subject can be induced to awaken during his dreams and, indeed, to become a conscious part of the dream itself and be able to control the dream. This a new field and very exciting! It allows someone to design any format, experience any sensation and to face any foe through dream control.

You can teach your subject that he will dream his problem out and become conscious of the dream and still remain in the dream and work the problem out. Tell him that when he decides to awaken he will have solved the problem completely. Depending upon how adept your subject is, he will have significant noticeable results and your efforts will be very beneficial.

The major disadvantage to lucid dreaming is that the person must control his own dream. Most of us are reluctant to conjure up fears and problems and when we control our own dreams, we will tend to being about pretty, interesting and generally innocuous dreams with little therapeutic value. Since the dream is very real and we are right in the middle of it, much fear and emotion may be experienced during this exercise.

CONCLUSION

This course is designed to allow the serious student to become involved in true therapy to a greater degree than ever before. It is preparatory to training in actual hypnotherapy followed by training in Hypnoanalysis.

When the student has mastered his skill and is ready, a course in Hypnotherapy, followed by Hypnoanalysis will tie everything together into a clear overall picture of how to discern a problem, deal with it and clear it with the highest degree of success possible.

The student must read current books, study the masters of old and apply training to practical applications on an individual basis. The student will master an understanding of the workings of the subconscious mind to a degree that few people in the world can comprehend.

ADDITIONAL BOOKS

And other information by:

Larry M. McDaniel

Change Your Words – Change Your Life

Faith, the Secret to Love and Success

Handwriting Analysis and Detection of Deception

Handwriting Analysis and Employment Screening

Hypnosis 101 – Basic Hypnotic Techniques

Hypnosis 201 – Advanced Techniques

Hypnotherapy 301 – Advanced Course

Hypnosis 401 – Hypnoanalysis - Psychothereapeutic Analysis

The Pemlar Profile – Employment Screening Test

LarryMcDaniel12@GMail.com